Natural
Selection

VISTA®
HIGHER LEARNING

Boston, Massachusetts

T0027197

Some animals are able to move very fast, other animals are able to **survive** despite moving very slowly. Some animals, such as the blue whale, are huge. Other animals are so small we cannot see them without help. Some animals eat only plants, while certain plants actually eat animals!

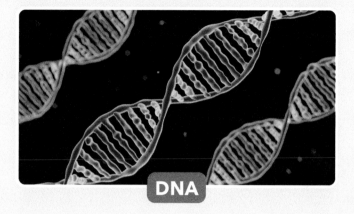

DNA

Why are living things so different? It's often because their **characteristics** have changed over time. How do plants and animals **adapt** like this? With the help of **DNA**.

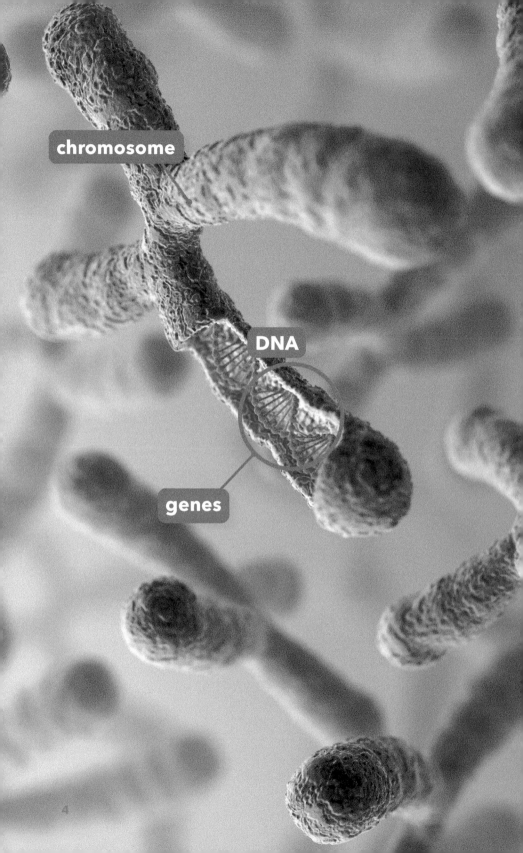

You can find DNA in almost all the **cells** of animals and plants. It holds the **genes** that give everything different characteristics over time. These genes sometimes change and give some plants and animals **traits** that help them survive. The survivors pass on these traits to their young. This is known as natural selection. Let's look at **the process of natural selection** and how different animals and plants have adapted.

beak

Three Kinds of Adaptation

Some scientists put adaptations into three groups: **structural** adaptation, **physiological** adaptation, or **behavioral** adaptation. Let's take a look at these three groups.

Structural adaptations are often the result of genetic **mutations**. For example, a mutation may give a bird a long beak. This helps the bird find food in the ground. As a result, the long-beaked bird will survive longer and pass on more of its genes. Other examples of structural adaptations are found in animals that live in cold areas. Some of these animals have a lot of fat, and others have long hair to keep them warm.

Physiological adaptations are changes that happen to an animal or plant as a whole. For example, animals like snakes are cold blooded. They need to live in warm areas to survive. Animals like

wolf

cactus (*pl.* cacti)

wolves are warm blooded. They are able to keep their bodies warm even in cold temperatures. This allows them to live in parts of the world where cold-blooded animals cannot live. Cacti have also adapted physiologically. They usually live in deserts and have adapted to survive a long time with no water. When it does rain, cacti are able to take in huge amounts of water. They can store this water in their cells.

Behavioral adaption is not a physical change but a change that involves an animal's actions. A good example of this can be seen in bears. Bears can live through long, cold winters when there is little food. They do this by sleeping more during the winter months. This allows them to survive in very difficult environments. For the same reason, some birds fly thousands of miles before the winter month. They do this to find more food and warmer weather.

These are wildebeests. They live in Africa and normally move slowly, but they can run very quickly when needed. An adult wildebeest can run up to 50 miles an hour (80 km / hr). A baby wildebeest can walk shortly after birth. It can run at just five minutes old. This is important for their survival. Why? Lions live in Africa, too. They're also very fast and are extremely powerful. Lions often follow wildebeests because they're excellent food for lions!

wildebeest

Wildebeests live in huge groups. There can be as many as 1.5 million of them living and eating together. Lions may attack at any time. When they do, only the wildebeests that have the trait for running fast can get away.

Another **inherited** trait that is important for survival is eyesight. In this case, wildebeest with better eyesight are more likely to see hunting lions quickly. They will move farther away from danger faster and live longer.

The wildebeests that survive for these reasons will pass on those genes to their young. Those that are caught will not. This is an example of natural selection or survival of the fittest.

lion

fur

Hares are small animals that are common in North America, Europe, Asia, and Africa. Many animals like to eat hares—if they can catch them. One problem for **predators** is that hares can run fast. They can also lie on the ground so that predators find it difficult to see them. Look at the color of this hare's fur. It's not easy to see a brown hare on the forest floor. The color of its fur helps to protect it from predators.

The arctic hare lives in the northern regions of Canada and Greenland where it is very cold and there is almost always snow. Look at the color of the arctic hare. Unlike its cousins farther south, it's white, not brown. Why? It's easy to see a brown hare in a snowy environment. It's more difficult to see a white one with the snow-covered background. Over time, the fur of some arctic hares started changing to white in winter. These hares were able to survive longer and pass on more DNA. Those with darker fur did not.

An octopus is a beautiful animal, but it's not a very fast one. Luckily, octopuses have developed special characteristics that allow them to survive. Some fish, like sharks, like to eat octopuses. How do octopuses escape from these predators? Natural selection has given them some tools!

First, octopuses have no bones. This means they can get into very small spaces where a predator is unable to catch them.

Second, octopuses have a special part of their body that can shoot ink. While the ink isn't dangerous, it does surprise the predator. This gives the octopus time to get away.

octopus

ink

shark

A third adaptation that helps octopuses avoid predators is the ability to change color if they are in danger. They use **camouflage** to look like the sea floor, which makes it difficult for predators to find them.

Octopuses have a behavioral adaptation as well. They have learned to cover their bodies with sand and rocks to hide themselves when a predator is near.

All of these things have developed over time to help more octopuses survive and pass on their DNA.

Fennec foxes live in the deserts of North Africa and the Middle East. It's not an easy place to survive! Temperatures are extremely high during the day. There is not much water and very little food. Only animals that have adapted to this difficult environment can make it here. How have fennec foxes adapted? They have changed in a few ways.

One adaptation is that fennec foxes have developed particularly large ears. This is important for two reasons. First, their large ears help them hear and locate small animals underground. As a result, they can dig down quickly to get food that many other animals couldn't. Second, these large ears help keep the foxes cool, which is very important for life in the desert.

Another adaptation is that, unlike other foxes, fennec foxes have fur on the bottoms of their feet. This protects them from the hot sand.

Fennec foxes have also adapted their behavior. They hunt at night when it's cooler. This allows them to hunt for a longer time. Fennec fox parents have passed on all of these traits and behaviors to their young over time.

Animals are not the only things that adapt. Plants also have genes and DNA that give them particular traits. For example, cacti have adapted to life in the desert. Most plants have leaves that can lose a lot of water. Cacti don't have leaves. Not having leaves means that cacti can live with less water. In fact, some can go without water for two years! The cacti that were able to survive in this difficult environment were also able to pass on more of their DNA.

The Venus flytrap lives in wetlands in the southern United States. Many plants cannot live in these areas. The ground is very wet, and they cannot get the nitrogen that they need to grow.

The Venus flytrap has adapted to this environment. It has special leaves that catch insects. It then produces chemicals that break the insects apart so the plant gets the nitrogen it needs to grow. The Venus flytrap adapted, and it now does well in an environment in which other plants could not survive.

Venus flytrap

nitrogen = the chemical symbol "N"

20

Every animal and plant on the planet has characteristics that help it survive. As environments change, so do the traits that are required to live there. Some plants have adapted to survive in new environments. Some animals have adapted to avoid being eaten. Some plants and animals have adapted to find better food sources.

Animals and plants are tested day in and day out to see which ones will make it. In this way, traits that are not suited to an environment are less likely to be passed on. Over time this leads to populations that are highly adapted to the environments in which they live. This is part of what gives us the incredible range of animals and plants that live on our planet today.

The process of natural selection helps nature decide which plants and animals will live on and which don't. The ones that are able to survive will pass on their DNA to the next **generation**. Each generation will be tested by its environment. Only the fittest will survive.

Extreme Adaptations

Natural selection affects all animals and plants on the planet. Some animals have adapted to their environments in extreme ways. Let's take a look.

African bullfrogs

African bullfrogs live in areas where it almost never rains. When it gets dry, the frogs bury themselves in mud. They can stay in the mud for up to seven years. When rain does come, they return to the surface. They can then feed, have young, and pass on those incredible genes.

Nicaraguan parrots

In Nicaragua there are a number of active volcanoes. Some of them give off dangerous gases. At least, they are dangerous to humans and most other animals. This kind of parrot has adapted to living inside the crater. The parrots seem unaffected by the gases coming up from below.

> *These changes are extreme. They are very big.*

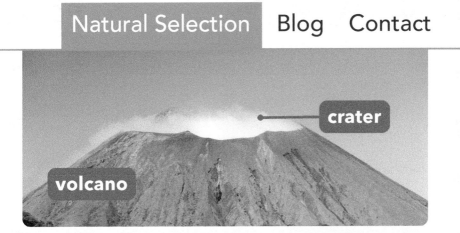

crater

volcano

Antarctic fish

The waters around Antarctica are very cold. So how do fish survive? Some kinds of fish have a special chemical in their blood. This stops their bodies from freezing. Without this adaptation they would not be able to live in such a cold environment.

Tardigrades

The tiny tardigrade is known for its extreme adaptations. Less than a millimeter long, tardigrades are found all over the world. They can survive temperatures down to -457.6 degrees Fahrenheit and up to 302 degrees Fahrenheit. They can go without food or water for 30 years. In 2007, tardigrades were even taken into space—and they survived!

32 degrees Fahrenheit = 0 degrees Celsius

survive to continue to live

characteristic a feature that is usual for a specific thing like a particular size, shape, form, or behavior

adapt to change in order to live longer or better

DNA (deoxyribonucleic acid) a chemical in a living thing that affects what it is like

cell a very small part in your body that makes up bigger parts

gene a very small part of a cell that goes from parent to young and that carries information about what that living thing is like

trait a quality that passes from parent to young, like eye color, hair color, body size, and so on

the process of natural selection a series of changes that allows one type of animal or plant to live longer or better than others

structural of or having to do with how something is made or built

physiological of or having to do with how the body works

behavioral of or having to do with how someone or something acts

mutation a sudden unexpected change in the very small part of a cell that controls what it is like.

inherit to get something from other family members or parents

predator an animal that eats other animals

camouflage coloring that allows an animal to look like its background in order to hide

generation a group of animals or plants that are about the same age